Contents

Introduction – An Unconventional View On Time Managements

Read a dozen books or blogs on Time Management, and you will almost always see the same conventional principles:

1. Create 'to do' lists
2. Prioritize
3. Avoid distractions
4. Don't procrastinate
5. Track your productivity and daily activities

And, while all of these can be quite true, they are mostly incomplete – and, sometimes counter-productive when done the wrong way.

They lack certain key and underlying principles that lead one to ask the questions:

Why is it that, even though we all have the same numbers of minutes in an hour, hours in a day, days in a week, etc., some of us accomplish and achieve far more in the same period of time than others?

Why are some of us able to 'get done' what needs to be done, while others are struggle and always seems be 'behind'?

Why do some people perform confidently, while others battle with feelings of being overwhelmed?

Of course, the answer is simply the difference in the way a person manages their time…

The problem is, most 'conventional wisdoms' of time management simply do not work. If they did work, everyone would be highly efficient and always productive beings – which, of course, a vast majority of the world isn't.

So, the key is to step beyond the text book definition of time management and apply principles that transcend the generic tactics commonly found.

This book isn't so much about tearing down conventional wisdom as it is about giving you key ideas and practical guidance towards being more efficient with your time and more effective with your results.

We will take you step by step through the concepts of distractions, health, dedication, focus, action, environment, multi-tasking, balance, and leverage.

Some of the concepts shared in this book will be unconventional – and, perhaps even unusual – in their relation to time management. However, if you are reading this book, you have likely found that 'convention' hasn't helped you become more productive.

These principles can be applied in all areas of life: schooling, work / career, home / family life, hobbies, and even social activities. And, while culture and technology may change, these principles are timeless – unaffected by change.

You can liken performance of time management to the performance of a professional athlete – especially, during high-pressure situations.

Some athletes are able to simplify the entire game / match into smaller, bite-size pieces. They focus on the next shot, move, pitch, throw, swing, stroke, step, or whatever else, rather than the big picture.

They are able to see the next course of action without being distracted by the audience, the competitors, or who's winning / losing. They don't get caught up in the anxiety of a moment, but rather focus on keeping their composure and channeling their adrenaline into the activity. They know that if they keep accomplishing the little things one by one, they are in a much better position to win.

If you look at 'closers' in professional baseball – a closer is usually the last pitcher to enter the game and ensure that his team wins – the best generally don't worry about the score, how many men are on base, and which batter they are facing.

These closers focus on the next pitch… and, then each subsequent pitch after that, one by one. They know that if they are successful on each individual pitch, everything else will sort itself out.

The same is true for the best golfers in the world. They generally tend not to worry about what their competition is doing, and instead focus on the next drive, the next iron stroke, or the next putt. They know that if their next shot is performed as best as they possibly can, then the following shot will be much easier to take.

Of course, professional athletes may also see 2 or 3 moves down the road, or even as much as 10 moves down the road – like a professional chess player.

However, the point is, they break the game down into simple, manageable segments that can be focused on then accomplished, like checking off a to-do list.

Successful professional athletes are also able to slow everything down – their perception of *relative time* changes as they slow their breathing, their heart rate, and quell any feelings of anxiety, fear, or nervousness.

Actual time moves at the same pace for everyone in the same location. However, *relative time* is based solely on one's perspective.

NOTE: There is proof that actual time does progress differently with relation to gravity and altitude. But, for the purposes of time management, let's focus only on a consistent environment.

When an athlete focuses on the next step and blocks out all other distractions, and when that athlete also focuses on maintaining composure, *relative* time seems to slow (even if only by fractions of a second); they're then able to react much more quickly to the situation and environment they're in.

While you may not be able to do this as well as, say, Michael Jordan, Derek Jeter, or Serena Williams, you can certainly practice the craft and develop the ability to effectively deal with high pressure (stressful) situations.

And, that right there is another thing the best of professional athletes do constantly… *practice.*

Whether or not they have an innate ability for their performance (something derived from their very physical / mental nature since birth or childhood), or they have had to work hard to get to peak performance, *EVERY* successful athlete has put hundreds or thousands hours into improving their abilities.

That's one of the KEY COMPONENTS to time management: you *NEED* to practice, repeat, and continue to develop your ability – it's not something that just happens.

Learning comes not just from reading or listening, it comes from action. The only way you'll improve your time management skill is to take action.

While planning and preparation are core components to developing time management and efficiency, they are meaningless without actually *doing* something. You have to *take action,* whether a big step or a small step, towards your goals. And, along with taking action comes refraining from making excuses.

Being *busy* is something that most people actually are – whether it's because of children, pets, multiple jobs, hobbies, household responsibilities, relatives needing care, or any number of reasons. However, "I'm busy," can many times be used just as an excuse, especially when there is a lack of motivation.

Some of the most productive people in the world are also the busiest. These people don't make excuses – they just focus on achieving results. They know that there's a personal responsibility and accountability to effectively managing their time; and, they know that it's not just their environment or the people around them that determine whether they are productive or not.

And, before we really dive into the factors that help create better time management, let's take a look at its main purpose.

At the end of the day, most of want to better manage our time in order to be more efficient and effective in our performance, as well as to increase our rewards (or, our reward time).

In other words, we want to better manage our time so that we get better grades, get the promotion and / or pay increase we've been hoping for, to achieve our goals, and to create a life that we want. We also want to increase our 'play time,' whether that means more travel, more freedom, more time do the activities we love most, etc.

So, our focus on time management is to be more effective with the time we have in front of us and more efficient with our performance of our tasks and duties.

With all of these points in mind, let's first start exploring the factors that negatively affect time management – factors which you should consider eliminating or reducing as you move forward.

Chapter 1 – Reducing / Eliminating Negative Factors

To be frank, the biggest obstacle to your own time management is *YOU*. This may come in the form of laziness, procrastination, self-doubt, denial, distractions, juggling too many tasks, or any other 'thing' that gets in the way of you accomplishing what you want / need to accomplish.

You are the one biggest thing standing in your own way of efficiency and effectiveness – and, as soon as you can come to terms with that, the more effective you will become.

Let's take a look at some of these factors and how you can personally remove the obstacle:

Taking On Too Many Tasks

There is a fine line between *effective* multi-tasking (discussed later) and biting off more than you can chew.

Ambition, while a very positive characteristic when it comes to improving one's success and accomplishments, can also work against you when it's left to run out of control.

This is where you need to be comfortable with saying "no."

When you take on too many tasks or activities at one time, it's hard to find a balance, and even more difficult to prioritize – especially, when they have similar time-frames or due dates.

Some people have a perspective that in order to accomplish more, you have to take on more responsibilities and duties. However, that's not necessarily true.

Sometimes, simplifying what's in front of you is the best way to accomplish more… in other words, many times, less is more.

Procrastination & Laziness

Let's face it, we're pretty much all guilty of procrastination at some point in our lives – whether it is schoolwork, housework / chores, job / career tasks, or other 'thing' we don't find very exciting or inspiring.

There are times where we simply can't be bothered to lift a finger to do a task or duty that is dull or boring.

As human beings, we're most motivated by things that stimulate our emotions:

Inspirational, fear of loss / failure, stressful, exciting, inciting love / passion, frustrating, creating desperation

These emotions drive us to do something.

And, the alternative depressants to our emotions, such as *boredom, tedium, monotony, resentment, and disgust* tend to anti-motivate us.

To combat procrastination, the first step is to recognize when you are actually doing it. Once you're able to recognize your moments of procrastination, you are able to take control and reduce or eliminate its detrimental effects.

The *ONLY* effective solution to overcome procrastination, regardless of what stimulation of emotions the task at hand gives us is to jump right into it – to *DO* something that works to accomplishing.

You have to take charge of yourself and move forward, even if it means only taking small steps towards your goals. Put yourself in motion – you'll likely find that your momentum will pick up over time.

Distractions

Human lives in the 21st century are mostly full of distractions: TV, the Internet, mobile phones, tablets, smart watches and exercise bands, billboards and road signs, advertising everywhere, a constant flow of information being sent to us over every platform, and a constant hum of technology, energy, and civilization humming in our ears.

Many times, we're overloaded with so much stimulation into our ears and eyes, that we can find it difficult to disassociate ourselves from the world around us.

But, that's what it truly takes in order to eliminate distractions and become more highly effective.

Going back to the successful professional athlete in the introduction, *most* successful athletes are able to completely block out distractions and focus on what is immediately in front of them.

We'll discuss focus more in a later chapter; for now, let's just start to eliminate the distractions that hold you back from your best time management – and, therefore, your best performance.

Depending on the task at hand, one *HIGHLY* effective way to eliminate distractions is to turn off all non-essential / non-relevant technology.

Perhaps, you need your computer or laptop in order to accomplish the task in front of you… but, do you need your mobile phone, which is likely constantly beeping, ringing, or flashing with notifications of social media, text messages, missed calls, and emails?

Get into the habit of turning it off (or, at least putting it in a desk drawer) for 30 minutes to an hour at a time. You may be surprised at how much more you accomplish when you're not looking down at the phone every 3-5 minutes to see if there's a new notification.

Eliminating The Negative Effects Of Stress & Anxiety

Before we talk about eliminating these two obstacles (or, at least reducing them), understand that based on our primal instincts that have developed over millions of years, our brains are programmed in such a way that it's difficult to take action until we feel some level of stress or anxiety.

We simply perform better when we're stimulated to act (in boredom and even in bliss, we can get lethargic).

And, of course, it's nearly impossible to eliminate all stress or anxiety in life.

Therefore, it's prudent to be able to simply manage our emotions and the *way we react* to stress and anxiety in our lives.

One important (but, sometimes challenging) way to start this process is to recognize when you're thinking or speaking negatively about yourself... then, eliminate it.

Self-degrading thoughts – such as, "this is too difficult for me," "I cannot do this," and "I am not good enough" – are counter-productive to being efficient and effective; and, they work against good time management.

Instead, focus on what you *can* do, even if it means breaking what you're doing down into smaller pieces. Also, remind yourself of what you *have done* in the past – a way to encourage yourself that you can do it again.

In addition, understand that plans change, things happen (such as distractions or obstacles). Don't be so hard on yourself when it takes a little longer to accomplish your goals. Instead, allow for it. Prepare yourself with extra time to accomplish a task at hand with the understanding that it will take longer than you originally plan.

And, finally, don't let the negativity of others bring you down. The people in our life, at times, may tell us that we *can't* do something, that it's impossible, or even that we're not good enough. Filter that kind of stuff out and don't let it get to you.

When you carry the world on your shoulders, it's more difficult to move forward.

Relax, take deep breaths, and focus on the step-by-step process to accomplishing your goals.

Chapter 2 – Health & Well-Being

You may not realize this, but your health and well-being play a large role in your ability to perform efficiently and effectively.

Proper sleep, nutrition, and hydration are important factors affecting your brain's ability to process information and your body's ability to perform necessary functions.

Therefore, it is prudent for you to start your time management process by ensuring that you're taking care of your health.

But, because you're unique, your personal health balance is something you will need to discover on your own – some people need more sleep than others; and, some people's dietary needs are different from another.

Sleep & Rest

Proper sleep is an important factor in productivity, efficiency, and effectiveness, as well as strategic thinking – all relevant to time management.

If you're lacking proper sleep, your ability to plan and perform will be far reduced from your optimal level.

In fact, according to WebMd, "Sleepiness can damage your judgment, work performance, mood, and safety."

This also includes taking breaks when needed. If you give your body and / or brain a chance to rest and refocus, you'll find that you can be much more productive during your activities.

The less sleep and rest you get, the less time your body and your brain have to recover. The worst part is, this can create a snowball effect:

If you are overtired, it can take longer to accomplish the activities and tasks you have in front of you. When you take longer to accomplish these activities and tasks, you have less time for rest. The less time you have for rest, the more overtired you become; and, the cycle continues.

In short, good sleep increases your attention span, concentration, creativity, decision-making, social skills, and overall physical and brain health.

Therefore, it's incredibly important to ensure you have time for rest (even in the form of small breaks) and time for sleep properly scheduled into your daily and weekly activities.

Nutrition & Hydration

When it comes to time management, ensuring that your body is properly fueled plays a large role in your ability to strategize, plan, and follow through.

In fact, according to an article in the Harvard Business Review, "Food has a direct impact on our cognitive performance, which is why a poor decision at lunch can derail an entire afternoon."

Remember that good food nourishes the body and powers the mind to be stronger. This also includes hydration – be sure to be consuming enough water (or, general fluids) in order to keep your body and your brain hydrated. You can also look into foods that empower your brain and your body to function better for the tasks you have in front of you.

A strong mind is better able to strategize (and, cope) with proper time management, and helps stimulate more efficient and effective performance.

A well-balanced diet, with the vitamins suitable for your own body's best performance is a key element to ensure that your mind is properly prepared for your day's activities.

This can (and, should) include small, healthy snacks throughout the day – whether cold vegetables, healthy crackers or bars, fruits, or even shakes and vitamin-enhanced drinks.

This also includes avoiding unhealthy foods, overindulging in high-sugar goodies, drinking unnatural energy drinks, and too much caffeine (which can cause a crash later in the day).

There are many nutrition resources available to you for free – or, you can consult with your primary physician for the best dietary alternatives for you.

Exercise

Whether you like to exercise or not, studies have shown that regular exercise helps stimulate the mind to better performance. The endorphins and the increased blood flow help stimulate body and brain function.

Conversely, a lack of exercise can incite depression and lethargy, both counter-productive to effective and efficient performance. An extended lack of exercise can eventually lead to either laziness or failing health (or, both). And, in the long run, neither will benefit you.

Therefore, ensure that you are scheduling some form of exercise into your daily and / or weekly routine. And, that does not necessarily mean going to the gym or running a marathon.

It can be as simple as taking the stairs instead of an elevator or escalator each day. It can include parking further away from the building, forcing you to walk a little further into school or work. Or, it can mean walking or taking a bicycle instead of a car or public transportation.

However you can work some form of physical activity into your daily routine, you will benefit immensely.

And, if your routine already includes daily exercise, keep it up.

Time of Day

First and foremost, every human being has an optimal working time frame. Some people work best in mornings, others during the afternoon, and still others in the evening and into late night.

Discovering your own optimal working time frame allows you to best schedule the tasks that matter most.

If you, for instance, work in an office from 8am to 5pm, with a 1 hour break for lunch, you're able to determine for yourself if you work best in the morning or the afternoon.

If it's the morning, simply work on the most intensive tasks before lunch and schedule all of your meetings, calls, and email responses for the afternoon. Or, perhaps the reverse is true.

In either case, it is best to *not* schedule the less-intensive activities – such as answering basic emails and returning non-essential phone calls – during your less productive times of day.

Surroundings & Location

For many people, a place of work or performance is a non-negotiable factor – such as if you're an athlete, performing artist, or work in a job that has a set location.

But, if you have the opportunity to move your working location, you'll be able to discover your optimal surroundings – especially, if you can change what you see and hear.

This may be as simple as moving your office around to change what you see when you look up from your desk. Perhaps, this means changing the location of your work space from one room to another. And, it could be as significant as changing your job entirely to a new company / location / position.

Only you can determine where you work best. And, *where* you work best is a significant factor in your time management efficiency and effectiveness.

If you can, try moving to an empty office, conference room, or classroom to see if you're more productive than your current location.

Our mind is stimulated by what we see. So, something as simple as hanging up a poster or picture of one of your favorite destinations, or of a scenic location (such as a tropical paradise, remote island, or mountain top) can create a subconscious feeling of peace each time you look at it.

In fact, you could even keep a picture in your back pocket of something that makes you smile or happy – pull it out when you need an extra bit of stimulation or inspiration.

Environment & Comfort Zone

This is one of the most important elements to time management and productivity – finding time to perform your tasks and duties in your personal comfort zone.

And, each person's comfort zone is unique… there is no cookie-cutter method to defining it.

But, there *ARE* elements to your comfort zone that can be defined in order to help you discover where and how you work best.

Noise (or, lack of noise) can play a significant role in your ideal environment.

Some people prefer to have music playing in the background or via headphones.

Others prefer white noise, such as the sound of waves, thunderstorms and rain, or simply static. Still others work best in complete silence.

While this is not always possible, any time you can manipulate the sound in our surroundings to your personal comfort zone, you'll find that your efficiency and effectiveness increase. And, when possible, schedule the most challenging of tasks and activities when you can place yourself in your own ideal noise environment.

You will need to determine for yourself which elements of both your location and what you see / hear in the background work best for you.

Keep in mind that your comfort zone is not limited to your surrounding environment – **it also includes your state of mind.**

An ideal environment is one where you're able to keep your mind in a state of drive and determination to accomplish. Finding a way to keep your mind focused on the tasks at hand without allowing distractions to interfere is incredibly valuable.

When you're able to place yourself in an environment that brings you peace of mind as well as encourages your motivation, you'll find you perform much more efficiently and effectively.

Keep Your Brain Fit

Studies have shown that a healthier and better-used brain can perform daily tasks better than a brain that's never challenged.

And, there's no exact science to this... but, as we reach our later 30s and move into our 40s, 50s, and 60s, our brain — just like our body — is not quite as strong, as quick, or as sharp as it once was.

Therefore, online brain training services, such as Lumosity, can significantly help your overall efficiency and effectiveness, as well as help you best strategize your time management.

Several studies have been published on a brain training's ability to improve key abilities such as working memory, visual attention, and executive function in people of different ages and from different backgrounds.

It centers on the principle of neuroplasticity: the brain is constantly changing in response to various experiences.

New behaviors, new learnings, and even environmental changes may all stimulate the brain to create new neural pathways or reorganize existing ones, and fundamentally alter how information is processed.

This is exactly what brain training intends to do:

It seeks to help your brain create new pathways by pushing your cognitive abilities above and beyond your comfort zone.

And, you'll find the more you practice, the more your brain is able to perform cognitive functions that may once have seemed challenging — thus, you've created more neural pathways and a better connection between your brain and your fingers on the keyboard.

Learn New Things

Much like keeping your brain fit, it's important to stimulate your brain with new processes (not just new information).

Whether it's learning a new language, a new game, a new concept, or a new way of doing something familiar, this sort of brain stimulation will keep your brain functioning.

When you learn something new, your brain actually changes – it forms new connections between neurons. And, it actually can help make other areas of your life easier.

Here are a few of the benefits of learning something new:

1. Learning across a wide range of subjects can assist in giving you a better perspective on what's immediately in front of you.

2. A broader knowledge can help stimulate new ways of thinking, trigger inspiration, and maybe even help you become more efficient at the tasks or activities at hand.

3. Learning can help you better adapt to the present situation.

Chapter 3 – Productivity

Understanding your own level of productivity will help you better define how to best manage your time.

Your productivity is simply how many tasks, activities, and actions you accomplish in a period of time – and, how well you accomplish those tasks, activities and actions.

When you're able to increase or enhance your productivity, you'll find that your workload will decrease, your output will increase, and you create the potential to have your income increase.

There are many ways to increase or enhance your productivity, and this book simply doesn't cover the full scope – however, here are a few tactics that can help you to be more productive

Don't Waste Your Own Time

As simple as it sounds, many people fall victim to their own time wasting. The amount of time one spends checking and re-checking social media, email, text messages, and other distracting influences is directly related to how productive that person is each day.

Stop Dwelling On Problems, Focus On Solutions

One of the best ways to be more productive is to focus your thoughts on how to overcome obstacles rather than ruminating on how the obstacles are interfering with your productivity.

The less time you spend worried or anxious about an issue, the more time you can spend productively resolving it.

There's A Difference Between Being Busy And Being Productive

People who are only concerned about being 'busy' tend to emphasize how busy they really are. Those who are productive find the time needed to accomplish the tasks and activities at hand.

People who are busy fill up their day with tasks that don't necessarily accomplish anything significant and rarely work towards their end goals.

Productive people take into consideration whether a task is going to move them toward their end goal, or if it can be put off in lieu of more important tasks.

Stay productive and work towards your end goals – being 'busy' many times just keeps you from accomplishment.

Practice Until It Becomes Second Nature

The old adage that 'practice makes perfect' – while not entirely true (perfect is nearly impossible) – is a core productivity concept that has scientific proof.

It's been said that to be an expert at something, you would need to dedicate roughly 10,000 to the trade or activity.

In fact, according to the Harvard Business Review, "Consistently and overwhelmingly, the evidence showed that experts are always made, not born."

And, while expertise may not be your end goal, your own proficiency at an activity lies somewhere in the middle of 0-10,000 hours. In other words, the more time you spend practicing, the better and more proficient become.

Get Feedback From Qualified Persons

Getting constructive feedback – and, even constructive criticism – from qualified individuals who are familiar and experienced with the tasks or activities you're looking to accomplish is a surefire way to improve your own performance and productivity.

The more productive feedback you can get, the better you can review your own performance and develop steps to improve it.

Just keep in mind that you're looking for a coach not a critic – the feedback should always be constructive, not degrading.

If you're unable to get direct feedback from a qualified person, you can take an indirect approach:

Compare your efforts to those of someone else performing the same activity (whether past or present).

By taking a look at factors such as time-to-complete, overall results, steps taking to complete, and quality, you can compare your performance to that of another person's, and make sure that you're being as efficient and effective as possible in your methods.

Just be sure not to spend too much time comparing your performance to others' – and, don't allow feelings of inferiority (if applicable) to infect your thoughts.

Just Do It

Sure, some tasks and activities take careful planning. But, avoid getting caught in a loop of preparation.

Instead, act. Do. Take charge of the situation and start working toward the goal.

Sometimes, it's easier to correct mistakes and errors during the process rather than spending an excess amount of time trying to be perfect.

Chapter 4 – Organizing, Planning, Scheduling, Prioritization

There's a fine line between proper balancing of organization / planning and going overboard with too much planning, which ends up wasting your time.

There are three keys goals to organizing, planning, prioritization, and scheduling:

1. To *DEFINE* what tasks need to be accomplished

2. To *DETERMINE* the order to accomplish these tasks

3. To *CREATE* a plan of action to accomplish these tasks

That's how simple this phase can be. When you get overly complicated with prioritizing or spend too much time planning, you can lose valuable time in the actual performance.

Therefore, it is important to be quick, precise, and efficient with the process.

The first step, of course, is to define what needs to be done. Create a list, if you'd like, of all the tasks you need to accomplish in the next day / week / month.

Be sure that you don't get caught in a mode of being a list maker.

Sometimes, we feel compelled to create 'to do' lists that simply tell us to do a prior 'to do' list. Or, we can spend so much time focused on *what* we need to do that we run out of time for actually doing it.

Keep yourself within reason and allow the list to live on its own over time – it will grow and contract as days or weeks pass, and as more tasks are added or accomplished.

The second step is to decide which are pressing and urgent, which are important, and which can be done at any point in time. Arrange these in a way that makes sense – the most pressing tasks first, important tasks near the top, and everything else near the bottom.

When you prioritize, take a moment to create a few if / then scenarios.

Be sure to take into account what it will mean if you don't accomplish a certain task right away.

Are there any drawbacks?
Are there repercussions?
Or, will everything be okay if it takes you longer to complete the task?

When you can weigh the costs and the benefits to completing certain tasks in a given period of time and then compare them to other tasks needing to be completed, you'll have a better understanding of which are of the highest priority.

Then, decide when / how you're going to accomplish these tasks. Many times, it's important to write this plan of action down: it's something you can refer to later on, it serves as a reminder, and it imprints some decisiveness into your mind.

Your plan of action can be as simple as a list of the order steps that need to be accomplished to as detailed as when, where, and how to accomplish these steps.

It's also very important to make sure you're scheduling in the proper rest, nourishment, and rewards throughout a period of time so that you're able to recuperate, recover, and maintain a high level of motivation.

Once you have the plan of action (or, 'to do list') in front of you, many times the general tendency is to do the easy work first and then work into the tougher tasks. Since we as a society generally seek frequent rewards or gratification, we like to check the simple stuff off the list first – it helps us feel like we've accomplished something as we see the bullet points being crossed off.

However, during that same process, we lose our ability to perform at our highest level once mental and / or physical tiredness starts to set in. And, when it's time to perform the more complex or challenging tasks, we're left either not having enough energy to complete it, having a bit of lethargy, which causes us to procrastinate, or simply putting it off until a later time.

Instead, try doing the opposite: tackle the most difficult tasks when you have the highest energy and allow your day to progress into the tasks and duties that require less effort as your daily energy drains.

Be ambitious.

Challenge yourself to accomplish certain things in a period of time. Force yourself to push your own bounds a bit. Allow for the opportunity to motivate yourself by creating a bit of pressure to complete your duties.

Keep yourself motivated by applying a small sense of urgency. And, be sure to keep your mind stimulated by keeping things moving.

However…

Be sure that you're realistic in your scheduling.

Sometimes, ambition can run a bit rampant, and we believe we can accomplish more than we will in a day. Ensure that you're allowing time for interruptions, corrections, and obstacles.

While we aim to be as efficient as possible, most of the time, we can't be. Allow for that. When you set forth realistic goals, you have a great chance of accomplishing them in the time period you set forth.

When you set unrealistic goals, you create the chance for failing to complete what you wanted – and, potentially set yourself up for disappointment.

There's a careful balance between a healthy, challenging schedule and that which is overloaded and overwhelming.

Try out the two-hour drill.

The two-hour drill works simply like this:

"If I have only two hours today to accomplish something or a few things, what would I do and why?"

You might be surprised that your order of priorities changes when you have only a limited time to accomplish the tasks or activities. It's a great way to cross-check your priority list.

However, keep in mind that the two-hour drill shouldn't take you more than a few minutes to complete. So, make sure you're not spending too much time in the cross-check process.

Chapter 5 – Focus

Focus is simply your ability to keep your attention and energy on a specific activity, goal, objective, task, or idea for a sustained length of time.

And, one thing is certain: you can CHOOSE to focus on your goals... or, to be distracted by the challenges and obstacles.

You can allow yourself to be overwhelmed by the big picture... or, you can keep the big picture in mind while you focus on checking off bullet-point after bullet-point on your list of steps to achieve your goals.

Sure, most success coaches and gurus talk about creating a 'dream board' and 'focusing on what you want in order to create your own reality'; but, many neglect to include the most practical (and, necessary) step, which is to create and organize a way to accomplish that goal piece-by-piece.

The key is to focus your attention on what needs to be done in order to get where you want — and, not allow the big picture to overwhelm you in the process.

And, when you combine this focus with taking action, you'll find that your life really does start to shift in the right direction.

Of course, this likely won't happen overnight.

It takes practice; it takes trial and error; and, it takes the occasional failure to learn and understand the next steps you may need to take.

If you stick to your personal plan and keep your focus, it's very likely that you'll find yourself much further along than you were before – and, you're much better at sticking to your time management plan.

Another useful practice to maintain focus is visualization. When you can visualize or imagine the results of accomplishing your goal(s) – whether it's the reward at the end, the sense of accomplishment, or the relief – it can be easier to maintain your focus on what you need to do.

Seeing yourself score the winning point, get a high mark on an exam or school report, or turn in the exact result your boss was looking for at work can create an extra sense of focus and diligence on the tasks in front of you. And, you can stimulate that sense by visualizing yourself after the task or activity in front of you has been accomplished.

This is what many successful professional athletes and performers do right before they act – they can see the result of their own success ahead of time and simply focus on the step(s) towards achieving that result.

This focus also serves the purpose of occupying your mind and preventing doubts, fears, and inhibitions from creeping in. When you lose focus, self-doubt can start to infect your thoughts… and, eventually, your performance.

Therefore, it's imperative to maintain your focus on your short- and long-term goals, on the end results, and then directly on the steps you need to take to accomplish them.

Chapter 6 – Self-Motivation, Self-Discipline, & Dedication

To be frank, how effectively you plan to manage your time is almost meaningless without proper motivation and discipline to follow through. If you're not dedicated to the plans to accomplish the duties and tasks in front of you, all the planning in the world won't make a single difference.

Therefore, it's highly important to maintain and nurture your inner self-motivation, self-discipline, and your dedication.

Let's face it: We're an instant gratification world. And, our brains are now (mostly) trained for immediate satisfaction and quick rewards – you can blame social media in part for that.

The good news is, there are various little tricks that you can implement to stimulate and encourage your self-motivation when it seems to be lacking.

So, one little trick that you can apply is to satisfy your need to be gratified for small accomplishments.

For instance, you can create mini-rewards for yourself for completing a stage of a task or duty – they can be as simple as a piece of chocolate for completing one page of a school report or work spreadsheet, to as rewarding as a much-needed vacation after completing an important career goal.

It doesn't matter how big or small the accomplishment or what the reward may be (so long as it pleases you), the key here is to simply create incentive for you to continue accomplishing the tasks / duties in front of you.

Slightly less ideal, you could also focus on what the negative result would occur if you do *not* complete the task(s) at hand. Perhaps the potential for a failed class in school, a loss of job, or other life-changing event may motivate you to complete what is in front of you.

Another approach is to stretch yourself and your mind by doing something complete out of your ordinary and comfort zone.

This is completely unrelated to the tasks you have in front of you; but, it provides a means of re-inspiring and re-invigorating your core through emotional, mental, and / or physical stimulation.

This could be as simple as brushing your teeth or combing your hair with your non-dominant hand. It could also be more challenging, such as walking or jogging a distance much further than you're normally comfortable.

Explore a part of your town, city, or village that you've never seen. Take a short weekend trip to a location you've never been. Talk to someone you've never interacted with on the street, on public transportation, or in your school or office building.

Do something that ignites your adrenaline or gets the blood racing – go see a scary or thrilling movie; climb to the top of a mountain or building; attend an exciting sporting event or any other of countless things that can fire up your internal energy.

All of these expansions of your personal comfort zone can trigger adrenaline and endorphins, which can reinvigorate your mind and spirit, and reignite the fire you need in order to press on with the tasks or duties at hand.

Take time to remind yourself and appreciate what you've accomplish to this point.

A good way to stay 'in the game' by staying motivated and dedicated is to remember your past successes – especially, when progress is slowed or it takes longer to achieve your next step than you had planned.

We sometimes get frustrated or disappointed by our failures (or, seeming failures), and this can reduce our drive to continue. And, this is when it's most important to focus on what you have accomplished and / or what you can accomplish next.

When you focus on your failures, you set yourself up for more potential failure. In fact, focusing on your failures and disappointments can and will cause you to *lose focus* on the more important things – such as your next steps and what you will achieve when you complete them.

Chapter 7 – Multi-Tasking

Multi-tasking is the ability to think about and perform multiple tasks, duties, or actions at the same time. You may be familiar with the concept of walking and chewing gum at the same time – that is a basic form of multi-tasking.

The issue with multi-tasking is that the conscious brain is unable to focus on one particular task or action at a time. If, while the conscious brain is focused on this one task or action, and the subconscious brain is not able to effectively perform the second task or action effectively (sometimes called, 'muscle memory'), then it could essentially take more time to complete both tasks together than it would to complete them one at a time.

Multi-tasking can also increase the likelihood of errors or mistakes if not done properly. When your attention is split into two or more directions at a time, there is an increased probability that steps or details will be overlooked – sometimes, without any awareness.

And, multi-tasking has been shown to use up brain energy more quickly than focusing on one task or action at a time. Therefore, fatigue can come into play, slowing down your ability to function efficiently and effectively until you get the proper rest.

But, the good news is that you can train yourself to effectively multi-task, especially through planning and preparation.

As your learn skills, your mind expands through more connections between your brain's neurons. And, as those connections get stronger, the less you'll have to think about what you're doing.

The less you have to think about what you're doing, the easier it is to multi-task.

One key element to practicing and training to multi-task effectively is to take notes, or keep a log / journal. Take notes of ideas that come into your head, but that will distract you from your current focus. And, keep a log / journal of what you've completed versus what you still need to complete.

These two activities alone will help you maintain organization without taking away brain energy during the time of performance and action. They will also help you ensure that you're not overlooking or missing any steps or details.

In addition, when attempting to multi-task, do your best to group similar and related tasks (or, at least, non-conflicting tasks) together. This will keep your brain from spending too much energy switching between thought processes.

Another tactic to multi-tasking is to combine tasks that don't use much brain power. The tasks that do not require your full focus, aren't prone to vital errors, and / or that are relatively simple allow you to multi-task with minimal risk of mistakes or failure.

You can also time your tasks so that you're filling in pre-planned breaks of one task within another task.

But, remember that the brain and your active concentration can really only focus on one thing at a time.

Therefore, it's best to focus on one task completely then switch to the next one and focus on it completely – even if you're working on both of them within the same time period.

If you switch back and forth two quickly, you risk mistakes AND you can drain quite a bit of brain energy. So, give yourself enough time to adjust your mindset to the alternating tasks, and don't put too much pressure on yourself to achieve too much, too quickly.

It's all about balance.

Chapter 8 – Leverage

One of the biggest key elements to effective and efficient time management is leverage. Leverage basically means doing a lot with a little to gain maximum advantage.

When you're able to combine not only your own efforts, but the efforts of someone or something (computer, machine, animal, etc.), you can gain another level to our output and performance that you wouldn't be able to achieve on your own.

Take, for instance, the example of a farmer:

A farmer has a large field and would like to plant a crop. Before planting, he needs to prepare the soil in the field by turning it.

To do this, the can use a hoe, dragging it for hours (or, days) by walking up and down the field.

However, doing it by hand is not the most efficient method, even if it is effective in creating the desired results.

As an alternative, the farmer could also choose to have a horse or oxen pull a much larger plough, which would significantly reduce the time it takes to complete the turn. This method is also effective, and it's much more efficient than dragging a small hoe.

A third alternative would be to use a tractor with a large plough on back. Just as the second alternative, this method is effective as well as much more efficient than the first method.

Both the second and third alternative are completed through leverage – leveraging either an animal or machine that can do far more work in a shorter time span than doing it by hand.

Or, let's take the scenario that you need to move your 'stuff' from one room to another (whether at home or at work).

You could move all of the furniture, decorations, and doo-dads yourself. Or, you could enlist the assistant of a friend, family member, or co-worker. Both would be equally effective – but, it's very likely that you'd be much more time efficient with the help of someone else.

As with the farmer who used an animal or tractor to turn his field, you'd be utilizing leverage and freeing up more of your own time in the process.

In some circumstances, you can consider which tasks may be able to be outsourced. Consider the cost (time) of doing it yourself versus the cost (money) of paying someone to do it for you.

Of course, some things are better done by yourself – but, many times you can pay someone to do the work for you, which allows your more time to accomplish what is important to you.

A simple example of this would be to pay someone to mow your lawn or clean your house. Another example of outsourcing is to pay a contractor to complete a report, article, or spreadsheet for you while you focus on other duties and tasks.

Still another example could include paying someone to answer emails and phone calls for you (such as a virtual assistant) to save you time in filtering out the priorities.

Outsourcing is a great way to leverage your time, allowing you to focus on core issues, while having someone else take care of the minor duties and tasks that take up your time.

But, leverage isn't just limited to the physical assistance of someone (or, something) else. You can also leverage another person's knowledge and experience – or, even the collective wisdom of many people.

Sometimes, the best way to complete a task or organize your priorities is by following the leadership of someone who has experience doing so. Other times, educating yourself through the knowledge of another person can increase your efficiency and effectiveness.

With the amount of information available today (via the Internet, among other places) on a seemingly limitless amount of topics, it's nearly always possible to be able to leverage off of another's person's knowledge and experience.

Wrap Up

Every hour has 60 minutes, ever day has 24 hours, and every year has 365 days – yet, it's clear that some people are far more productive within the same period of time than most of the rest of the world.

If you're like most of the world interested in learning more about time management, it's usually because you want to be more efficient with your time and more effective with your results.

The best way to achieve this is to take a step beyond the conventional lessons and practices of time management and understand each of the following:

No One-Size-Fits-All

No matter what conventional wisdom or the text books say, there's no one perfect method for time management. Just as every human being is unique, perception of time and skill sets are also unique to each individual person.

Therefore, it's important for you to discover your own unique method of time management based on an adaptation of what you've learned today. Take control of your own efficiency and effectiveness by finding your own comfort zone and optimal environment for performance.

Be Responsible & Accountable For Your Own Results

Taking responsibility for your own output and results is the best way to become more efficient – by accepting that you're accountable for your own actions (or, lack thereof) you're able to better assess what you can and cannot accomplish within a certain period of time.

Practice Makes ~~Perfect~~ Better

Learning proper time management is not an instantaneous result. It takes practice, diligence, and dedication.

Practice helps us complete a task while using less and less active brain processing and energy – it makes actions more automatic and allows for the better potential of effective multi-tasking.

With time management, the more you work on refining your process, the more you repeat these actions, the more you practice, the more adept you will become at it.

Take Care Of Your Temple

The health of your body – and, more specifically, your brain – is a vital factor in maintaining your best efficiency and effectiveness in your activities.

Do your best to ensure proper blood flow, sensory stimulation, nutrition, and hydration throughout each and every day.

Exercise regularly, learn something new frequently, and participate in mental exercises (such as brain training) that will help your mind continue to perform at its highest potential.

Ensure that you're getting the proper rest and sleep that your body needs to function properly. And, take regular breaks.

Stay Positive

Prevent negative thinking and avoid thoughts such as, "I can't do this," or "I don't have enough time."

Negativity is a huge obstacle that can prevent you from your most efficient and effective performance.

Keep your eyes on the prize and remember to look back and appreciate what you've already accomplished.

Keep Your Focus

Whether it's on the end goal or on the small steps to get there, keep concentrating on what matters most – what you're looking to accomplish.

Reduce or eliminate distractions (including distracting thoughts) whenever possible. And, as best you can, avoid allowing the unimportant things to draw your attention.

Use Leverage When Possible

As the Beatles once famously sang, "I get by with a little help from my friends…"

And, while it may not be your *friends* who assist you, they were definitely onto to something:

Any time you can utilize the assistance of someone else (where the benefits outweigh the cost) – whether physical, intellectual, or emotional – you'll find that you're able to accomplish far more than you can on your own.

Keep Yourself Motivated

Find ways to keep yourself 'in the game' when you find your ambition and motivation running lower.

There any many ways to keep yourself motivated, including: *rewarding yourself for small achievements, reminding yourself of past successes, visualizing future success, and stimulating your adrenaline through exciting or engaging activities.*

Find the ways that work best for you and keep yourself energized when you engage the less-than thrilling tasks.

Stay Productive Not Busy

There's a big difference between being productive and being busy. Focus on tasks, actions, and activities that get you towards your end goals, rather than tasks that simply occupy your time.

The more productive you are, the better you can make use of the hours in a day.

The Bottom Line

Proper Time Management starts and ends with you – and, it's only as good as its implementation.

All the planning in the world won't make a difference if there's no follow-through.

You are your best tool towards achieving efficient and effect performance – and, you are your best asset when managing your time.

www.ingramcontent.com/pod-product-compliance
Lightning Source LLC
Chambersburg PA
CBHW070338190526
45169CB00005B/1947